Lerner SPORTS

EXTREME SPEED

SUPERFAST RALLY CAR RACING

J Chris Roselius

Lerner Publications ◆ Minneapolis

Lerner Publications Company
An imprint of Lerner Publishing Group, Inc.
241 First Avenue North
Minneapolis, MN 55401 USA

For reading levels and more information, look up this title at www.lernerbooks.com.

Main body text set in Myriad Pro.
Typeface provided by Adobe.

Library of Congress Cataloging-in-Publication Data

Names: Roselius, J Chris, author.
Title: Superfast rally car racing / J Chris Roselius.
Description: Minneapolis : Lerner Publications, [2020] | Series: Extreme speed (Lerner sports) | Includes bibliographical references and index. | Audience: Ages 7–11 | Audience: Grades 2–3 | Summary: "Start your engines and get in gear! Full-color photos and engaging text will have readers turning the pages to discover the history of rally car racing, what a typical race day looks like, and more"— Provided by publisher.
Identifiers: LCCN 2019026104 (print) | LCCN 2019026105 (ebook) | ISBN 9781541577206 (library binding) | ISBN 9781541587397 (paperback) | ISBN 9781541582941 (ebook)
Subjects: LCSH: Automobile rallies—Juvenile literature. | Rally cars—Juvenile literature.
Classification: LCC GV1029.2 .R67 2020 (print) | LCC GV1029.2 (ebook) | DDC 796.7/3—dc23

LC record available at https://lccn.loc.gov/2019026104
LC ebook record available at https://lccn.loc.gov/2019026105

Manufactured in the United States of America
1 – CG – 12/31/19

CONTENTS

CHAPTER 1

CLIMBING THE HILL

Some rallies take place in forests. Others take place on snowy mountains or in dry deserts.

During the summer months, many people drive up the scenic Mount Washington Auto Road in New Hampshire. The summit of Mount Washington is 6,288 feet (1,917 m) above sea level. Cars pass through clouds as they make their way up to the top. The drive up the mountain is not easy. The air is thin and the narrow road can be slippery. There are no guardrails to protect drivers from the steep drop-offs. One wrong move can be deadly.

FACTS AT A GLANCE

- A rally can last one day or multiple days and covers special **stages** of the road.

- Rally cars go from 0 to 60 miles (0 to 97 km) per hour in less than four seconds and can reach speeds up to 125 miles (200 km) per hour.

- If a rally car suffers major damage on the road, the driver and **co-driver** must be skilled enough to fix it.

- The Race to the Clouds is a race in Colorado that starts 9,400 feet (2.9 km) up a mountain and goes to the summit at 14,199 feet (4.3 km).

It usually takes at least 30 minutes to drive up the winding 7.6-mile (12.2 km) route. But Travis Pastrana is not an ordinary driver. In 2017, Pastrana conquered each twist and turn in an incredible 5 minutes, 44.72 seconds, setting a new record. The previous record was 6 minutes, 9.09 seconds, set by David Higgins in 2014.

People can drive themselves to the summit of Mount Washington or they can take a guided tour to the top.

Some early rally cars did not have roofs. This made it dangerous for drivers if debris flew into the car.

The Mount Washington Hillclimb has been an event since 1904, making it one of the oldest racing events in the United States. Yet it's just one of many famous rallies around the world. Fans have been watching rallies for decades because of the extreme speeds and times achieved on courses. In the 1970s, fans cheered as Sandro Munari won his third Monte Carlo Rally in a row. And in 2012, Sébastien Loeb broke the record for most World Rally Championship titles when he crossed the finish line at Rally Catalunya to the screams of his supporters.

Some rally sections overlook steep drop-offs. Drivers make sure that their cars handle the tight curves.

Rally racing, or rallying, is a race over closed sections of real roads or off-road courses. The cars are basically the same vehicles millions of people drive each day, with a few **modifications**. Many people consider rallying to be one of the most exciting forms of racing.

A rally can last one day or multiple days and covers special stages, or sections, of the road. Stages can be from 1 to 25 miles (1.6 to 40 km) in length, with a typical rally covering 10 to 20 special stages. Most rallying events are 100 to 200 miles (160 to 320 km) long. Making the race even more exciting is the fact that drivers must maneuver over concrete, gravel, dirt, mud, snow, ice, or a combination of these terrains and conditions.

Because Rally Sweden takes place during the winter, drivers must navigate ice and snow-covered roads.

The Yalta Rally in Yalta, Ukraine, is part of an amateur rallying event called the International Rally Challenge.

The World Rally Championship (WRC) organizes rallies around the world. In the United States, the American Rally Association (ARA) is the top organization for stage rally events. Rally teams compete in different classes, and the drivers, co-drivers, and teams compete for national championships by earning points based on their position when they finish each rally of the season. First place in an ARA rally is awarded 22 points, second receives 17 points, and third gets 14. The team with the most points after the final race of the season is crowned the champion.

Rally Italia Sardegna provides fans with maps of the road stages. Devoted fans can use the maps to find great spots to view the race.

CHAPTER 2

RALLY CARS

Rally cars can lift off the ground when they speed over obstacles and hills.

The Rally Show Santa Domenica takes place in Croatia. Ninety European teams participated in the race in 2019.

All rally cars are built to race. However, they must be street legal. This means that they can drive on city streets because they have the correct parts, such as exterior lights. They must also be registered and insured.

Cars competing in the top WRC classes meet certain requirements. Each car has a **turbocharged** four-cylinder engine. Cylinders are engine parts that use pistons to generate power. The more cylinders an engine has, the more powerful it is.

Some classes allow for engine modifications, but all cars are allowed to upgrade their **suspension** and tires. A car's suspension system helps absorb the energy created by bumps and holes in the road. Without this suspension system, it would be difficult to control the car and keep it on the road.

Dust and dirt can make it difficult for the driver to see. Fortunately, the co-driver's notes can help him or her navigate the terrain.

Rally cars have strong suspension systems and tires. These help them drive easily over hills and on slippery surfaces.

ARA competitions have Four-Wheel Drive (4WD) and Two-Wheel Drive (2WD) classes. In 2WD cars, power from the engine goes to two wheels to move the vehicle forward. In 4WD vehicles, power goes to all four wheels. This gives the 4WD vehicle twice the grip and gives the driver more control.

WRC cars must be 4WD and weigh at least 2,620 pounds (1,190 kg) without the driver and co-driver. They go from 0 to 60 miles (0 to 97 km) per hour in less than four seconds and can reach speeds up to 125 miles (200 km) per hour.

When a crash causes a rally car's wheels to bend, the car becomes undriveable and the team may be knocked out of the race.

Because rallying is dangerous, there are many safety features to protect drivers and co-drivers in case a crash occurs. Rally cars must have a **roll cage** to protect the driver and co-driver if the car flips over. Inside each door, rally cars have foam that absorbs the impact of a crash. Parts of the car's **body** are also reinforced to prevent debris, such as tree branches or fence posts, from entering the car through the door.

Competing at the highest level can be expensive. The cost of an engine alone can be more than $200,000. Fully built rally cars can cost close to $1 million. Amateur drivers who are new to rally racing may spend $10,000 to upgrade suspensions, wheels, lights, and safety equipment, and to add a roll cage, new seats, and new seat belts.

REALLY?!

The WRC Volkswagen team built crates, costing $34,000 each, to transport the team's cars to each international rally. The giant crates allow the cars to be transported on nearly any plane. The cars can be flown back to the headquarters in Germany from anywhere in the world in about 48 hours.

CHAPTER 3

PREPARING TO RACE

Some races feature narrow bridges, steep hills, and muddy tracks.

Teemu Suninen (*right*) and his co-driver Jarmo Lehtinen finished in second place in the 2019 Rally Italia Sardegna in Italy.

Rally races can be held on a wet road, a muddy trail, or a course covered in snow. Drivers must handle tight turns and bumps on all types of courses. Because of these extreme changes and conditions, rally drivers are some of the most skilled in the world.

Due to the long days spent in the car, drivers need to stay fit. Driver Teemu Suninen runs and rides his mountain bike to exercise between races. He also makes sure to get the right amount of sleep before a race.

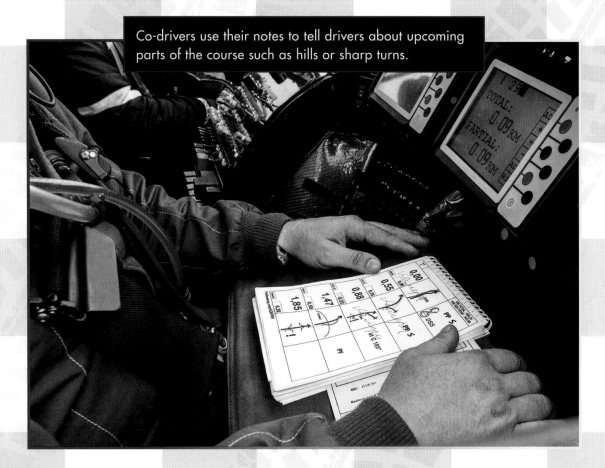

Co-drivers use their notes to tell drivers about upcoming parts of the course such as hills or sharp turns.

The driver doesn't have to do everything on her own during a race. Unlike many other forms of car racing, rally racing features a co-driver. Before each rally, the driver and co-driver get to drive the road at legal speeds. This is called a **reconnaissance** run. The co-driver takes notes about the course.

The reconnaissance run is not the only way drivers and co-drivers prepare for dangers on the road. They also have lots of safety gear. Drivers and co-drivers wear fire suits in case they get stuck in a burning car. They also wear helmets, safety harnesses, and seat belts to prevent injuries.

The pit crew practices before the rally too. Time in the team's **service area** is limited. In the WRC, cars can only be in the service area three times and only for a certain length of time. The first service can last only 15 minutes, the second is 30 minutes, and the final one is 45 minutes. The pit crew needs to work carefully and quickly to get the car back on the road.

REALLY?!

When a rally car slides through a turn sideways, it is not by accident. This is known as drifting. The driver makes the car go sideways on purpose. This allows the car to get the most grip on the road and exit the turn as fast as possible.

CHAPTER 4

IT'S RACE DAY!

Fans at rally courses wave banners in support of their favorite drivers.

Thanks to technology, rally fans can follow the sport at any time. The ARA has location tracking and timing equipment on all competitor vehicles. Fans can follow an ARA rally in real time, seeing where each driver is on the road and the times of the other racers.

However, attending a rally in person is one of the most exciting things a race fan can do. Spectators not only get a chance to be close to the road, they can meet their favorite racers and even get their autographs.

Nearly every rally begins with the Parc Expose. This event usually lasts for a few hours. All of the teams and cars gather in the same location. Teams often give away posters and other items. Fans meet the drivers and touch the cars. All of this builds excitement for the rally.

Some stages of Rally Sweden take place in the dark. Drivers must use their headlights and other safety features to navigate the terrain.

Cars begin the rally one or two minutes apart. Previous rallies determine the order of the race. For example, on day one of Rally Sweden, the first car to leave the starting line is the team that won the previous race, the Monte Carlo Rally. However, on the second and third days of racing, the team in last place for the day during Rally Sweden goes first, and the cars leave the starting line in reverse order.

The cars do not race each other at the same time. Instead, they are trying to get the fastest time for each section of the race. At the end of the rally, the times are added together to find the winner of the race.

PROFILE IN
SPEED

DAVID HIGGINS. David Higgins has dominated rally racing in the United States since 2011. A member of the Subaru Rally Team, Higgins won six straight Rally America championships from 2011 through 2016. He earned 28 rally event wins during that time, including all eight Rally America events in 2015. In 2018, he also claimed the American Rally Association title.

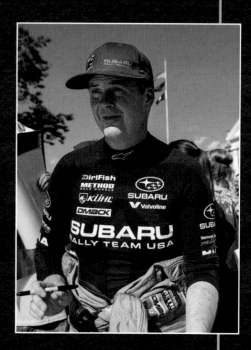

During the race, the co-driver tells the driver about upcoming turns, the length of a certain straightaway, or places where the surface of the road may change. If a car suffers major damage on the road, the driver and co-driver must be skilled enough to fix it. Otherwise, all repairs to cars are made at the service area, which is away from the stage area and often out of sight from fans. Typically three or four stages will be held before the car is allowed to go to the service area.

Co-drivers help drivers navigate turns where fans may be standing close to the road.

In the United States, one of the top rally events is the Pikes Peak International Hill Climb in Colorado. Also known as The Race to the Clouds, the event was first held in 1916. The 12.42 mile (20 km) road features 156 turns and climbs from approximately 9,400 to 14,100 feet (2.9 to 4.3 km) at the summit. The thin air on Pike's Peak can affect the driver's mental and physical strength. It also affects how the car engine burns fuel. By the end of the race, engines can lose up to 30 percent of the power that they had at the start of the race.

One of the top races in Europe is the Monte Carlo Rally. This is the first race of the WRC season each year. The rally takes place in the Alps, a mountain range in central Europe. Drivers must expect snow and ice while conquering tight turns and driving on asphalt.

The future of rally racing may change dramatically. Some experts speculate that soon races may feature electric or even self-driving cars. But one thing is for sure: whatever form they take, rally cars will conquer off-road action and race at top speeds from start to finish.

At the Monte Carlo Rally, fans can walk around and view current and previous rally cars before the race.

RALLY CAR
FAMILY TREE

Rally cars have changed drastically over the years, but one thing has stayed the same—they're made to go fast!

Brian Culcheth, 1970s

Carlos Saintz and Luis Moya, 1980s

Colin McRae and Nicky Grist, 2000s

Cevdet Alptürk and Mustafa Yucener, 2010s

GLOSSARY

body
the main section of the car that the other parts attach to

co-driver
the navigator in the passenger seat who tells the driver about directional changes and road conditions ahead

modifications
changes

reconnaissance
a period before the race where drivers and co-drivers can map out the track

roll cage
a structure of high carbon steel tubes welded inside the passenger compartment designed to keep the driver and co-driver safe in an impact or rollover

service area
an area or garage where the pit crew can repair the rally car between stages

stages
the competitive sections of the rally, also called special stages, where drivers and co-drivers drive as fast as they can to complete the section in the shortest time possible

suspension
the parts of a rally car, including springs and shock absorbers, that hold the tires to the body of the car

turbocharged
boosted power, achieved by forcing extra air into the engine cylinders

FURTHER INFORMATION

American Rally Car Association
https://www.americanrallyassociation.org

Bowman, Chris. *Rally Car Racing*. Minneapolis: Bellwether Media, 2016.

Levit, Joe. *Auto Racing's G.O.A.T.* Minneapolis: Lerner Publications, 2020.

Red Bull: 7 Ways You Can Get Started in Rally
https://www.redbull.com/gb-en/rally-driving-how-to-start

Wonderopolis: How Does an Engine Work?
https://www.wonderopolis.org/wonder/how-does-an-engine-work

World Rally Championship
https://www.wrc.com/en

INDEX

PHOTO ACKNOWLEDGMENTS

The images in this book are used with the permission of: © Jack Taylor/Getty Images News/Getty Images, p. 4; © Taras Vyshnya/Shutterstock.com, p. 5; © sebastienlemyre/Shutterstock.com, p. 6; © Haynes Archive/Popperfoto/Getty Images, p. 7; © Francisco Amaral Leitao/Shutterstock.com, p. 8; © Corepics VOF/Shutterstock.com, pp. 9, 24; © maxpro/Shutterstock.com, p. 10; © Lpuddori/Shutterstock.com, p. 11; © EvrenKalinbacak/Shutterstock.com, pp. 12, 29 (bottom right); © Goran Jakus/Shutterstock.com, p. 13; © Afsin Celik/Shutterstock.com, p. 14; © Sabri Kesen/Anadolu Agency/Getty Images, p. 15; © Hugh Peterswald/Icon Sportswire/Getty Images, p. 16; © Pascal Pochard-Casabianca/AFP/Getty Images, p. 18; © Andreas Solaro/AFP/Getty Images, p. 19; © Manamana/Shutterstock.com, p. 20; © Octavio Passos/Getty Images Sport/Getty Images, p. 22; © Brett Carlsen/Getty Images Sport/Getty Images, p. 25; © Nacho Mateo/Shutterstock.com, pp. 26–27; © Pierre Jean Durieu/Shutterstock.com, p. 28; © Barry James Gilmour/Fairfax Media Archives/Getty Images, p. 29 (top left); © Leo Mason/Popperfoto/Getty Images, pp. 29 (top right); © Andy Butterton/PA Images/Getty Images, p. 29 (bottom left).

Front Cover: © D Primrose/Alamy.